> Lawerence & Kimberly,
> I pray this encourages you in faith during this stormy season
> DSM

Reflections of Hope

COURAGE TO FACE YOUR FEARS AND
MOVE TRIUMPHANTLY FORWARD

Darryl S. Moore

PURE PRAISE PUBLISHING
P.O. Box 4012
Southfield, Michigan 48037

Reflections of Hope
Turning Your Dreams into Realities
Copyright© 2008 Darryl Moore

Unless otherwise stated, all Scripture quotations are from
The New International Version
Copyright © 1982, by Thomspon Nelson Inc.
All emphasis within italics are the author's addition.

ISBN 978-0-9740877-4-0

All rights reserved under International Copyright law. No part of this book may be reproduced or transmitted in any form or by any means; electronic, mechanical, including photocopying and recording, or by any information storage and retrieval system, without permission in writing from the publisher.

Cover Design and Layout: Larry T. Jordan, Pure Praise Media
Editing and Proofing: Tracy Flaggs

Published by:
Pure Praise Publishing
P.O. Box 4012
Southfield, Michigan 48037

Printed in the United States of America

Table Of Contents

Table Of Contents	III
Dedication	V
Introduction	VII
Forward	IX
Acknowledgements	XI
A Unique Seat	1
Bearing Witness	5
Being There	9
Climate Change	13
Dealing with Difficulty	15
Encouraging Yourself	17
Excellence Avoided	21
Facts, Fear and Faith	23
Feeding your Hope	27
Headed in the Wrong Direction	29
Holding on to Hope	33
Is It in You?	35
A Seat At the King's Table	37
Knowing Him	41
Letting Go and Moving Forward	43
Listening is An Act of Love	47
More Than You Expected	49
On Peace	53
Patience	57
Staying on Track	59
Singing Your Song	61
Surrender	63

Tablet of Contents continues on page IV

Table Of Contents Continuation

Taking a Nap	67
Test Time	71
The Faith Factor	73
The Mount Carmel Blues	75
The Power of One	79
The Roundabout Way	83
The Second Half	87
Like Home	89

Dedication

To My Parents

(Pops) Ennis Lanier Moore Sr. (1925-2001)
and Elizabeth Moore

for providing hope and inspiration to
their eight children
w
And
Miss. Nia Khemet Moore
(The Daughter of Daughters)

Introduction

Stony the road we trod, bitter the chastening rod,
Felt in the days when hope unborn had died;
Lift Every Voice and Sing, James Weldon Johnson

We have this hope as an anchor for the soul, firm and secure.
Hebrews 6:19

Have you ever felt that there is no reason to hope? Has life become a series of one disappointment after another? Or have you looked into the distant horizon and felt that nothing will change in the future? These feelings could be because you have received a layoff notice, experienced the loss of a loved one, loneliness, depression or a devastating illness, or been betrayed by a spouse or confidant.

I know that in these moments life seems to have no rhythm, meaning, or purpose. Chaos and confusion invade our inner spirit. Life is spinning precariously out of control and you seem to have no ability to steer yourself back onto the straight and narrow highway of life. We are left with a feeling of desperation.

Hope, when it is crushed, even before its birth leaves a life devoid of meaning. I know because I have been there. It is against that backdrop that these writings have taken shape. In the last several years I have experienced body blows that seemed to be unbearable at the time. The pain of these blows occurred through the loss of my father, divorce, the passing of a dear friend and the disappointment of leaving pastoral ministry. But God has given me grace to not only survive, but to thrive in the face of life's challenges.

It is common to the human experience that disappointment comes by to visit each of us. In those moments we wrestle with feelings of isolation and loneliness. This often leaves us feeling that you have been picked out by God to be picked on. I believe that as you read the pages of this book you will find that you are not alone in your experiences. No, they are quite common and visit each of us on one level or another. I believe that as you journey with me for thirty days, you will find the courage to face your fears and move triumphantly to a new place of spiritual renewal.

I began writing these devotions three years ago for the members of Third New Hope Baptist Church in Detroit, Michigan. I was encouraged by my good friend, Dr Reginald Blount, to use my writing skills as a way to help others see God's transformative power in everyday life situations. I shared this thought with Pastor Edward L Branch, who expressed his support for this creative endeavor. The response from the beginning was very encouraging from members of the congregation. Eventually, I began to share them with family and friends who insisted I put them in a book to reach others for Christ.

I want to encourage you; that though you may have received many blows, they have not been fatal. You have been blessed by God to hold on just a little while longer. God has provided you with strength to endure and stay in the race. I pray that as you read these devotions that they will help to anchor your spirit in Jesus Christ. *Shalom.*
DSM

Forward

As the deer pants for the water brooks, so my soul thirsts for God... (Psalm 42:1-2)

What the soul needs is intimate time with God. This is the meaning and purpose of personal devotions. It is really about having a devotional life. It is not something to happen occasionally or sporadically, but continuously. It is the devotional life that quenches the thirst of a longing soul.

Darryl Moore has tapped into a most precious part of ones spiritual life. Through a series of clear and precise devotional messages he leads the people of God to streams of refreshing waters sufficient to meet the needs of the soul. While many Christians are serving in ministry, fulfilling their duties and meeting deadlines; they are also suffering internally because of an undeveloped devotional life.

Along with a regular diet of teaching and preaching, regular worship experiences with a family of faith, and engaging in an area of service, there is a need for believers to spend private time with God in personal devotions. Often we assume that this is happening for everyone when many of us are negligent in this area.

I join with Reverend Moore in encouraging each of

us to use these devotions as a path to a stronger walk with God and may each of us find a new level of power for ministry and for our daily lives.

Edward L. Branch, *Pastor*
Third New Hope Baptist Church
Detroit, Michigan

Acknowledgements

I would like to express my warm and sincere thanks to the following people for providing hope in my life.

My Village: My siblings - Larry, Dianne, Joanne, Beverly, Neicy, Champ and Duane. My Extended Family - Aunt Bet, Doc (Hank), Dort, Keir Sabbath, David Jones, Mr. & Mrs. Sylvester Jones, Mom & Pops Felder, Anson Rhodes, Ronal Moore, Gloria and Lucille Tarvin, Reverend Barbara Woodson and Dr. Sharon Kennedy Collins (gone but always in my thoughts).

Spiritual and Intellectual Mentors: Reverend Harold C. Huggins (my father in ministry), Reverend Albert D. Tyson III (for modeling the power of the Christ in preaching), the late Dr. Fredrick G. Sampson, Dr. Charles G. Adams, Dr. Patricia Coleman Burns, Dr. Michael Eric Dyson, Dr. William Banfield, Bishop Edgar Vann and Pastor Everett Jennings, Sr. (my big brother in the faith).

Prolific Proclaimers: Reverends Andre L. Spivey, Anthony Hood, Christopher Martin, Felecia Thomas, Kenneth James Flowers, H. Michael Lemmons, John Harvey, Donald Lutas, Drs. Monica Coleman and Michael C. Carson.

Friends for Life: Sheila Abrahams, Paula Brinston, Mike Mayberry (we're in the trenches), Rob J (Mac), Tracy Flaggs, Freda G Sampson, Keith Harris, Eleanor Walker M.D., Dr. Reginald Blount (the professor), Tara Adams Washington M.D. (for the many challenging early life intellectual conversations), Brian Page, Mike VT (thanks for your guidance in this process), Kevin Troupe, Reverend Charles Christian Adams (my brother) and Dr. Trunell D. Felder (my best friend in life).

Churches: St. Stephen A.M.E. Church-Detroit (there is no place like home), St. Stephen A.M.E. Church-Chicago, Third New Hope Baptist Church (and the wonderful Ministry Team of Christian Education and its students), Hartford Memorial Baptist Church (and the mighty men of the Tuesday Night Bible Study), Scott United Methodist Church (thanks for having me as your assistant pastor), Serenity Christian Church and New Faith Baptist Church International.

Thought Shapers and Editors: Reverend Joy K. Challenger, Tracy Flaggs, Rosemary Sharpe and Paula Brinston.

Photography: Freda G. Sampson (you da girl)

Publishing: Thanks to Pastor Larry Jordan and Pure Praise Media.

Special Thanks to Pastor Edward L. Branch for your care, comfort and concern; and for preaching that inspires me to seek the depths of God for my life.

Day 1

A Unique Seat

And David went up and lived in the strongholds of En Gedi.
1 Samuel 23:29

Last week I had the privilege of attending my first Detroit Red Wings game in a suite at the Joe Louis Arena. I was amazed at the speed and ability of the players as they skated, changed directions, and shot the puck. The home team won the game 5-0 but sitting high above the ice caused me to appreciate my unique position watching the game.

This was not my first time watching a sporting event from the comfort of a suite. The suite offers special perks that regular seats do not. In order to get to your suite you usually have to go through an extra layer of security. You first show your tickets upon entering the arena and then you display them again as you enter the suite level. You see, the suite tickets cost more because there are extras that you receive that are not available to those who have the less expensive seats.

In the suite, your sight lines are very clear. You don't have to worry about somebody jumping in front of you and obscuring your view. There is nothing worse than missing an important play because the person in front of you insists on standing throughout the entire game.

Day 1 | A Unique Seat

Life is lived in the arena. We are not isolated in living but must come in contact with other people and situations. Sometimes these people are rude and irritating and do everything possible to harass us, thus causing stress. Then there are those whose actions are intentional to hurt and maim us. It is extremely painful when we find the person that is attempting to hurt us is a close friend or member of our family.

It is in these moments that we need to flee and escape to a place of sanctuary. The scripture reading tells of David running and seeking refuge. He was on the run simply for doing his job and doing it well. His boss Saul is envious and jealous and wants to take David's life. The place he went to is called the stronghold.

Strongholds historically are places of armed fortification. Strongholds were often looked at as being impenetrable. Often they were in high and lofty places which gave the occupants of the stronghold the ability to look down on those who were planning an attack. Castles in medieval times were strongholds.

In modern warfare, the Maginot Line, a defense system constructed by the French after World War I to defend against Germany, is an example of a failed stronghold. In the Second World War, the German blitzkrieg ran a decoy maneuver and sent a rear guard to the surprise of the French. Paris was captured a few days later.

David's position was spiritually sought and ordained by God. It did not come because of personal wisdom or strength, but because he inquired of God to provide him a place of safe haven. David was responsible not only for himself, but six hundred men as well. Saul as the king, leveraged his influence with the people of the neighboring towns in an attempt to kill David.

If you take the time to read the entire Chapter of I Samuel 23, you will find that God constantly put David in a position to observe the advance of his pursuer and keep him safe from danger. This is because David sought God's counsel.

A favorite verse of mine is Isaiah 26:3, "You will keep in perfect peace him whose mind is steadfast, because he trusts in you." I believe this verse moves the believer to a state of mind to understand that God is able to lift us to places of safety and security and provide for all our needs. God will do this even in the midst of personal attacks and life's trials.

Day 2

Bearing Witness

But Peter and John replied, "Judge for yourselves whether it is right in God's sight to obey you rather than God. For we cannot help speaking about what we have seen and heard."
Acts 4:19-20

It is common in life that we focus on our own pain. The pathos of our own conflicts seem to be the only issue in the universe. We are wrapped up by our lives, which very rarely allows us to hear or see the pains of others. Today, I would ask that we turn our focus outward instead of inward.

Jesus' disciples were just like us in many ways. They struggled with issues of ego and self-esteem as James and John maneuvered to sit at Jesus' right and left hand. They wanted their own private club to be exclusionary when observing another man who was not part of their circle doing ministry. They could be angry, insolent, self-absorbed, scared and doubtful.

An amazing thing happened after Pentecost. Their focus began to change and they moved forward in ministry. Peter and John healed a man in the name of Jesus and the crowds followed them. The religious leaders were upset and told them not to speak or teach in the name of Jesus. They declared that they could not stop speaking about what they had seen and heard.

It was not only the ravages of Hurricane Katrina that caused

Day 2 | Bearing Witness

me to come back and bear witness to my trip, but also the many reminders of the plenty that many of us enjoy while others go with so little. However, let's start with N'awilins, if you will. Over 2000 persons died or are missing in the Gulf region. There are close to a million households that were displaced by Katrina. The conference was housed at a hotel in the historic French Quarter. However, most of New Orleans continues to remain uninhabitable and uninhabited.

I also sat in a workshop on The Church and Global Witness. The facilitator helped us to understand that just as oil is a precious commodity, so is water. Over one billion of the world's people do not have access to safe water and 2.6 billion do not have adequate sanitation. In addition, almost 20% of the world's population still lacks access to safe drinking water.

I would finally ask that you turn your thoughts not to Iraq, but to Africa. We were privileged to have ministers who have traveled to Darfur where genocide is occurring and 400,000 people have been killed. Three and a half million people are completely reliant on international aid for survival. Two million people have been forced from their homes into refugee camps. This does not take into account the savage beatings of the men or the horrific rape of women and children. In addition, of the 40.3 million people living with HIV; two thirds are in the Sub-Sahara. In the absence of a medical miracle, nearly all will die before 2010.

I could go on by telling you of the 12 million U.S. adult residents who have been homeless at some point in their lives, the three billion people of the world who live on less than $2 per day, or that 1.2 billion people in the world that suffer from hunger. I recently heard my Pastor say in a recent sermon that if you talk to someone else about what they are going through your life would seem like a picnic.

I pray that you understand that this does not minimize your pain when you are going through a trial. I do pray that while you bear witness to the goodness of God in the sanctuary through your praise, it will also cause us to bear witness outside the sanctuary.

There is an often used quote of a 19th Century British statesman, Edmund Burke, that says "The only thing needed for evil to persist is for good people to do nothing." I believe that the Spirit of God in us will cause us to pray and praise; bear witness to the Christ and change the world around us.   Shalom.

Day 3

Being There

God said to Moses, "Climb higher up the mountain and wait there for me (be there, NKJV); I'll give you tablets of stone, the teachings and commandments that I've written to instruct them."
Exodus 24:12, The Message Bible

I was fortunate growing up to have Godparents that owned a motor home. I traveled with them throughout the United States and saw the Sleeping Bear Dunes in Northern Michigan, the Mammoth Caves in Kentucky, the Amish Country in Pennsylvania and many other wonderful experiences to numerous to name.

A motor home has all the conveniences of home on wheels. A camper no longer needs to contend with sleeping in a sleeping bag, cooking over a fire, or hauling water from a stream. Now he can park a fully equipped home on a cement slab in the midst of a few pine trees and hook up to a water line, a sewer line and electricity. Motor homes can even be equipped so that you can receive ESPN, HBO and Cinemax in the middle of nowhere. No more bother with dirt, no more smoke from the fire, no more drudgery of walking to the stream. Now it is possible to go camping and never have to go outside.

One buys a motor home with the hopes of seeing new places and getting out into the world. Yet, we deck it out with the same furnishings as in our living room. Thus nothing really changes. We may drive to a new place, set ourselves in new surroundings, but

Day 3 | Being There

the newness goes unnoticed, for we've only carried along our old setting.

We have been challenged in our Lenten reading, "Treasures of a Transformed Life," to leave our old settings or patterns and begin to live anew or deepen our relationship in Christ. The adventure of new life in Christ begins when the comfortable patterns of the old life are left behind.

Last week, during our teaching pastor for the fall revival, John Schmidt of the Frazer Memorial United Methodist Church in Montgomery, Alabama, mentioned the above passage of scripture and it caused me to reflect deeper on its meaning for transforming our lives.

Moses has begun the ascent up Mount Sinai. God speaks to him and tells him to climb a little higher up the mountain. A necessary step for transformation is to go a little higher than your present altitude. Often in our walk of faith we become comfortable; plateau, if you will, because we are doing so much better than we did previously. We stop and become satisfied without realizing that God is calling us to so much more.

Then God tells Moses in the NKJV to "wait there" or "be there." Pastor Schmidt observed that it is possible to be there and not be present. It is the same as someone asking, "Do your hear me?" This question is an observation that you are hearing, but not listening. Possibly this is where we get the old adage "In one ear and out the other." I see listening as an active engagement of the hearer with the speaker. It speaks of a symbiosis between the two. The listener is wrapped up in the thoughts of the speaker in a way that the two become one.

    When we become so wrapped up in being in God's presence we place ourselves in a position to receive instruction for the journey ahead. I believe that God is always speaking, teaching, advising and doling out wisdom. The problem is we continue to scurry back and forth, ignoring or not listening to His counsel. Today, take a moment to "be there." It just might change your life.

Day 4

Climate Change

Before Isaiah had left the middle court, the word of the Lord came to him. "Go back and tell Hezekiah, the leader of my people, your father David, says I have heard your prayer, and seen your tears I will heal you.
2 Kings 20: 4-6

It is often said if you don't like the weather in Michigan, just wait a minute and it will change. Yes, climate, age, health and fashions will all change. Someone once said, "Life goes through changes so fast, you think your life is great, then one of your best friends dies. Then, you think you found someone you truly love, only to figure out, she doesn't love you back. You cry and cry and cry, but nothing changes. You realize, that you must accept things for what they are, and what they have made you become.

Everything in life changes you in some way. Yes, even the smallest things. If you do not accept these changes, you do not accept yourself. For through these changes brings new and greater things, making you wiser, as time progresses. To avoid these changes is a loss. You only live your life once. Do not waste a minute of it avoiding things. Let them come to you, and learn from them. There's always tomorrow.

The promise of tomorrow was surely not comforting to King Hezekiah. He was ill and close to the point of death. He had been told by God that he was to put his affairs in order. Death would be soon and sudden.

Day 4 | Climate Change

It was at this point that Hezekiah turned to the one constant in an ever-changing world. He called on the name of the Lord. We are not told how long he prayed or where he prayed or what his posture in prayer was; we only know that Hezekiah prayed. Prayer should be a regular and constant communication with God. We should pray without ceasing. Pray when we arise and when we go to sleep. We should pray.

I would like to encourage you-that if someone you love has died, a great love in your life has ended or this morning finds you in tears, I want to encourage you to stop right now and pray. I cannot tell you what or how long to pray. Pray and believe that the one constant in life is God. He is the same yesterday, today and forever. (Hebrews 13:8)

God not only heard Hezekiah pray and saw his tears, but he sent a word of affirmation. He promised that he would heal him, add fifteen years to his life, and deliver his people from foreign oppression. I believe that as you pray God is causing the climate to change around you even if you cannot comp,rehend or see it.

Like the weather in Michigan, just wait a minute, the climate will change.

Day 5

Dealing with Difficulty

In those days Hezekiah became ill and was at the point of death. The prophet Isaiah son of Amoz went to him and said, This is what the LORD says: "Put your house in order, because you are going to die; you will not recover." Hezekiah turned his face to the wall and prayed to LORD.
Isaiah 38:1-2

An old woodsman gives this advice about catching a porcupine: "Watch for the slapping tail as you dash in and drop a large washtub over him. The washtub will give you something to sit on while you ponder your next move." Life seems to present us with one set of difficult circumstances after another.

The difficulties of life when piled on top of each other often push us to the point of desperation. We then consider "throwing our hands in the air," "burying our head in the sand" or jumping in the car and driving away, never to return. However, after careful consideration, we become clear that none of these is a serious option.

We are further perplexed because our own analysis of ourselves would indicate we are good people. That being the case, we don't understand why God allows us to be pushed into such awful situations.

Hezekiah's plight was very similar to our own. As king of

Day 5 | Dealing with Difficulty

Israel, he had undertaken many reforms and attempted to turn the people's hearts back towards the Lord. He is described in scripture as a king who had a close relationship to God.

When Hezekiah's illness moves him towards death, he makes several important steps that could be important as he deals with his difficulties. He makes a radical departure from his normal prayer life. He turns his face to the wall as a display of extreme and total dependence on God.

God observes our cries and pleas; however, we are blessed that he does more than that. God saw the bitterness of Hezekiah's tears and hears his request to be remembered. He then speaks through the prophet Isaiah to tell the king that the same God that was with David will be with him. God would add fifteen years to the king's life.

When facing life's difficulties, it is good to remember we can depend on God. It has been said, "Since God has put His work into your weak hands, look not for long ease here: You must feel the full weight of your calling; a weak person with a strong God."

Day 6

Encouraging Yourself

David was greatly distressed because the men were talking of stoning him; each one was bitter in spirit because of his sons and daughters. But David found strength in the LORD his God.
I Samuel 30:6

I have been a University of Michigan football fan since I was seven years old (Sorry MSU readers). As a child, I felt the world was coming to an end if Michigan lost to Ohio State in the last game of the season. The results of football games are not as important to me now as they were then, but I still like to see my favorite team win.

I, like most maize-and-blue followers, was totally horrified when the team lost to smaller division Appalachian State, and then embarrassed on national television a week later to Oregon. Sports columnists, callers to sports radio, and alumni called for the firing of Coach Lloyd Carr. Carr, at a press conference after the Oregon loss, was asked tough questions but refused to wilt under pressure. He simply jutted his jaw, and in summary, told everyone that he would prepare his team to play the rest of the season.

Last week Lloyd Carr resigned as the head football coach at the University of Michigan. He did what he said he would do: he prepared his team to play. They won eight straight games before losing to Wisconsin and Ohio State (ouch). He was hailed by all as a man of integrity and character.

Day 6 | Encouraging Yourself

This caused me to think about how to handle life when you are the constant source of criticism. I am sure that someone reading this feels the pressure of a spouse that is never satisfied with your cooking, level of income or the ways you express intimacy. Perhaps your family criticizes you because of where you choose to live, or you have a supervisor who picks apart your best work.

David was under criticism from his own men that had followed him in war. They returned to the city where they left their wives and children, to find it had been captured and everything had been burned to the ground. When things go bad someone has to bear the brunt of the blame. The soldiers all looked at David and pointed the finger at him. The men wept until they had no more strength. Their frustration now centered on David. The talk led to discussions of stoning him to death. Martin Luther King Jr. said, "The ultimate measure of man is not where he stands in moments of comfort and convenience, but where he stands at times of challenge and controversy." David was in uncharted waters.

He could have easily ran, given up hope, held a pity party or blamed everyone else. Instead, we are told he found strength or encouragement in the Lord his God. The text does not tell us how, but let me give you a suggestions. He remembered what God had done for him. When facing the Philistine giant Goliath, David recalled that God had given him victory over the lion and the bear. (I Samuel 17:37) If God did it then he could do it again.

I believe that remembering what God did in the past reminded him that his strength was in God and not in himself. I am sure that when you look at how you got a job that others seemed to have an inside position on, or a home that you did not have the credit score to get, you realize it was God's strength and not your own.

When the Michigan football program was 0-2 after being a preseason top five pick, there were fans that wanted to stone Coach Carr. At a press conference he was asked how he was handling all the criticism and the rumors he might be fired. Carr paused, and then spoke about a kid named Peter who had sent him a short note of encouragement. And through the cameras and the microphones, he answered that kid:

"I'm doing great," he said. "I've got great kids here. And you don't know me. But those who do know me, friend and foe, I think would agree that I'm a tough-minded, competitive guy. And there isn't anything that comes my way that I can't handle, professionally. And there is nothing, there is nothing that can keep me down. Not a loss to Appalachian State, not a loss to Oregon. Not a hundred losses. And not the loss of my job...."

You're probably going to lose a lot of games the next few years. And my advice to you is when you lose, don't make excuses, don't blame your coaches or teammates or the officials. Just play every day as hard as you can. And regardless of what the outcome of those games,, are, you keep your head high. Because if you're doing everything you can to the best of your ability, you have nothing---nothing---to be embarrassed about.

Keep your head up, trust in God, find your strength in Him and get back in the game. *Shalom.*

Day 7

Excellence Avoided

As they were walking along the road, a man said to him, "I will follow you wherever you go." Jesus replied, "Foxes have holes and birds of the air have nests, but the Son of Man has no place to lay his head. He said to another man, "Follow me." Jesus said to him, 'Let the dead bury their own dead, but you go and proclaim the kingdom of God. Still another said I will follow you, Lord; but first let me go back and say good –by to my family. Jesus replied, No one who puts his hand to the plow and looks back is fit for service in the kingdom of God.
Luke 9:57-62

A major theme of our church is "A Spirit of Excellence". It is quite easy to list a roll of those who have attained excellence. Luciano Pavarotti, Dr. Benjamin Carson, Dr. Martin Luther King Jr., Vincent Van Gough, Oprah Winfrey, John F Kennedy, Mary Mcleod Bethune, Thurgood Marshall, Condoleezza Rice, Albert Einstein, Mother Theresa, Tiger Woods. There is a common thread in each of these individuals that sets them apart from every one else. It is their desire to give their very best.

Excellence has many definitions. Perhaps this example will help. The name Stradivarius is synonymous with fine violins. This is true because Antonius Stradivarius insisted that no instrument constructed in his shop be sold until it was as near perfection as human care and skill could make it.

Stradivarius observed, "God needs violins to send His music

Day 7 | Excellence Avoided

into the world, and if any violins are defective, God's music will be spoiled." His work philosophy was summed up in one sentence: "Other men will make other violins, but no man shall make a better one."

Each of the individuals in Luke's narrative had an opportunity to move towards excellence. Instead, they chose the path of least resistance. They found excuses instead of striving for excellence. Their avoidance of difficulty rendered them as would-be disciples.

Seeking excellence does not mean that your name will be immortalized in the pantheons of history. No, it simple means that you and I will strive to do better today than we did yesterday. The legendary football coach Vince Lombardi stated, "The quality of a person's life is in direct proportion to their commitment to excellence, regardless of their chosen field of endeavor.

I believe excellence for the Christian means embracing the fullness of the potential God has placed in us to change and transform the world around us.

DAY 8

FACTS, FEAR AND FAITH

On the evening of that first day of the week, when the disciples were together, with the doors locked for fear of the Jews, Jesus came and stood among them and said, "Peace be with you! After he said this, he showed them his hands and side. The disciples were overjoyed when they saw the Lord.....Now Thomas (called Didymus), one of the Twelve, was not with the disciples when Jesus came. So the other disciples told him, "We have seen the Lord!" But he said to them, "Unless I see the nail marks in his hands and put my finger where the nails were, and put my hand into his side, I will not believe it."

John 20:19-20, 24-25

The large majority of us live our lives based on what we know. We can easily account for the money in our bank account or the degrees we have earned or the influential friends we can call on if we are stuck in a jam. However, there are occasions where the things that are supposedly verifiable are thrown into disarray by the contradiction of the moment. For example, my daughter was excited because the calendar and the weatherperson said it was the first day of spring. This should mean sunshine and warmer temperatures. Instead, the current weather contradicts that which should be verified fact.

The disciples observed that Jesus can do that which was impossible. Jesus turned water into wine at Cana of Galilee. He feed multitudes of men, women and children on two different occasions. He raised Lazarus and the only son of widow at Nain

Day 8 | Facts, Fear and Faith

from the dead. Jesus gave the disciples power to cast out demons and any evil that stood in their way. This caused them to come back with joy and give a good report to Jesus of their newfound spiritual power. The next day shows a different story.

The tables have turned on the disciples and they are confused, frightened and fearful. Fear will put your life on hold. The disillusionment caused by the death of a loved one, medical reports that show your body failing, divorce or corporate downsizing can cause us to give up on ever realizing the potential of a brighter tomorrow.

I am sure I am not the only one that has experienced the grip of fear. It is in these moments that we feel as though God has forgotten us and life has dealt us an unfair hand. The pain of the moment causes us to only perform the most basic task necessary to make it through the day.

Jesus understood the dilemma of his disciples and shows up in their midst. His appearance brought a sense of renewal, refreshment and revival for those that he loved. Thomas was not there and spoke to his disbelief by uttering that unless I see the evidence, I will not believe that the Lord has risen.

Yes, the fact is that we want proof. The state of Missouri's motto is, "The Show Me State." This is where many of us are. We are like Thomas, except he had the blessing to see Jesus in the midst of his unbelief. So you ask, "how I can move beyond the pain and predicament of my present existential situation.

First, look up. Someone once said, "That when you straighten up your shoulders no one can ride your back." Look downing is reflective of your mental and spiritual state. I would have you simply think of the words or terms associated with down. Downcast, downtrodden, downturn, down and out all speak to a sense of hopelessness. When I look up, I see God and begin to consider and realize the possibility for change.

Why? It is because I look to God who is the Creator and Sustainer of the Universe. God looked at the void of the universe and spoke everything into existence. The world asks me to prove it. I respond by saying that I live by faith. This is ignorant to the unbeliever but pleasing to God. (Hebrews 11:6) The facts speak to fear and failure, but faith speaks to favor and fullness. The facts speak to doubt and despair, but faith speaks to vitally and victory. I suggest instead of looking at the facts, look to God in faith.

DAY 9

FEEDING YOUR HOPE

Why are you downcast, O my soul? Why so disturbed within me? Put your hope in God, for I will yet praise him, my Savior and my God.
Psalm 42:5

Last week a visiting pastor (Pastor J) blessed my church family with a powerful message, "Lord You Are," during our pastor's anniversary revival. In her sermon, Pastor J raised the very important point of "feeding your hope." We have all experienced moments, times and places where hope seems to have taken a vacation. I would like to share some thoughts today that might assist you, whether you are in the throes of despair, or disappointment is outside your front door but has not knocked yet.

In order that the craving of the human spirit is nurtured we must find a reservoir of strength in our weakness. The hunger is often deep and unyielding. It is in these times that we have to manage our emotions. Often there is no other outlet except to talk to yourself. The Psalmist was clear that his spirit was in disarray and he could not quite put his finger on the problem. I am sure that there are times you know exactly what's wrong and others where a self-diagnosis is necessary. We can-with God's help-put our finger on the issue, but the proper prescription is needed for healing.

We should then turn our attention towards heaven. The

Day 9 | Feeding your Hope

Psalmist says "Put your hope in God." We must turn to the Unseen Seer. God's omnipresence is upon every living creature and we can be confident that he cares for us. He has given us a model in Jesus that has experienced the turbulence of life and defeated every enemy, even death itself. Jesus did this by relying on the Word of God (Matthew 4:4) and constant communication with his Father (Mark 1:35).

When we continue to praise God in our lowest moments I believe this provides a foundation for miracles to become manifest in our lives. The end of this verse addresses God in a two-folded manner. The former describes his ability to pull us out of and deliver us from the depths of our despair. The latter term describes his power to "call those things that were not as though they were." (Romans 4:17) We can believe God and trust him in each and every situation.

Our situations can be compared to a little leaguer whose team was having a rough day. A man approached the boy and asked the score. The boy responded, "Eighteen to nothing—we're behind." "Boy," said the spectator, "I'll bet you're discouraged." "Why should I be discouraged?" replied the little boy. "We haven't even gotten up to bat yet!" Feed your hope, God hasn't gotten up to bat for you, yet.

DAY 10

HEADED IN THE WRONG DIRECTION

But Jonah ran away from the LORD and headed for Tarshish. He went down to Joppa, where he found a ship bound for that port. After paying the fare, he went abroad and sailed for Tarshish to flee from the LORD.
Jonah 1:3

During my pastoral ministry, one of my nephews would ask me almost weekly if I would preach about Jonah. Jonah, for some unknown reason, had become his favorite biblical character. Today, I'd like to journey with Jonah.

It is stereotypically suggested by many that men will not stop and ask for directions. Instead, it is often said that the male species would rather continue driving around making one turn after another than seek assistance. This supposed stubborn streak leaves them often going in circles, as opposed to asking for counsel from others.

I will share with you that I am not one of those men, but the analogy certainly speaks to the situation of our lives, too often. We have taken off and have no clear sense of how to arrive at our intended destination. We could very simply ask God and he would bring us safely to our desired end.

Jonah's situation is slightly different, but likewise frustrating.

Day 10 | Headed in the Wrong Direction

Jonah is given a clear directive by God. He is called to travel to the city of Ninevah and preach a message of repentance. Jonah goes in the opposite direction. The people of Nineveh exploited the helpless, plotted against God and participated in idolatry and witchcraft. (Read the OT book of Nahum). This helped Jonah come to the conclusion that the Ninevites were beyond saving.

We, often like Jonah, hear and receive God's Word and it gives us clear directions to live fruitful lives. We sometimes run because we believe God's way is too difficult or he is asking too much of us. We head in the wrong direction and become lost. Then like the stereotypical male driver, we are embarrassed and won't seek directions to make it back to safety.

I would have you consider early in this New Year, that running causes us to find more trouble. Pastor Branch suggested in a recent sermon that for each day that we go against the grain, it will take us that many days in the wrong direction, plus the same amount of days to retrace our steps. So if you go 100 miles in the wrong direction, you then have to cover the same distance to get to the point of origin, and then began to move towards your desired goal. You can apply this principle throughout your life. Think about it as you settle in for that late night ice cream or the Krispy Kreames tomorrow morning.

I would simply suggest that in whatever area of our lives that we are seeking improvement, it would be easier to listen to and follow God's direction. It does not matter how smart we think we are or how many degrees we have attained, when we are left to our own devices, we usually get lost in life.

Headed in the Wrong Direction | Day 10

There is a story of Albert Einstein on a train. Everyone in his car recognized him and knew who he was. Prior to the train leaving the station, the conductor made his routine inspection to ensure that each passenger had their tickets. The conductor noticed Einstein fumbling through his things, in his pockets, and papers. When the conductor reached him, Einstein admitted that he had lost his ticket and could not remember his stop! "That's no problem Mr. Einstein," the conductor replied, "We know who you are." Einstein responded, "I know who I am too, but I do not know where I am going!"

If we were to tell the truth, many people in life do not know where they are going; let alone what God's purpose for them is. I pray that you will avoid the aggravation of wasting time and energy on wild goose chases. God is still willing to direct the path of those who seek him with a willing heart.

Day 11

Holding on to Hope

We wait in hope for the LORD; he is our help and our shield. In him our hearts rejoice, for we trust in his holy name. May your unfailing love rest upon us, O LORD even as we put our hope in you.
Psalm 33:20-22

The act of waiting is like a foreign language to modern culture. We have become accustomed to almost everything being done in an instant. This causes frustration for many of us when we believe that an action should be completed quickly, fast and in a hurry. Someone said, "The ability to calm your soul and wait before God is one of the most difficult things in the Christian life. Our old nature is restless...the world around us is frantically in a hurry. But a restless heart usually leads to a reckless life."

The Psalmist understood our impatience. He encouraged Israel in tough times to wait and hold on in hope. Warren Wiersbe suggests that "Waiting for God is not laziness. Waiting for God is not going to sleep. Waiting for God is not the abandonment of effort. Waiting for God means, first, activity under command; second, readiness for any new command that may come; third, the ability to do nothing until the command is given."

I believe that as the Psalmist invoked hope in the LORD, it reminded the people of God who He is. If they needed any explanation, he told them first that God is our help. Each of us has experi-

Day 11 | Holding on to Hope

enced turning to a friend or family member for assistance in a time of crisis, only to be disappointed. God is an ever present help at all times and in all places.

He is not only a help but also a shield. I saw a You Tube video of a 92 year old woman in Tennessee who was being robbed at gunpoint in her car at a Wal-Mart. She told the would be robber that Jesus was always with her and that He was in the car at that moment. The man stopped his robbery attempt as the woman began to pray for him. I would say that God was a shield for her.

The chaos of life may have caused you to almost give up hope. It has been said that there are no hopeless situations; there are only people who have grown hopeless about them. I urge you ... no matter how desperate your situation ... to hold on to hope. Help is on the way.

DAY 12

IS IT IN YOU?

Moses answered the people, "Do not be afraid. Stand firm and you will see the deliverance the Lord will bring you today. The Egyptians you see today you will never see again. The Lord will fight for you; you need only to be still."
Exodus 14:13-14

On a recent road trip, I stopped at a gas station. I went inside to pay for my gas and to purchase a beverage. I chose Gatorade as opposed to a Coke or Pepsi. I did not choose the regular Gatorade but the specialty drink "Tiger." As you may know, the marketing slogan for Gatorade has been "Is It in You?" So I guess drinking this Gatorade was supposed to invoke the spirit of Tiger Woods in me. When I got back on the highway, I gave an enthusiastic double pump of my fist, like Tiger does after sinking a clutch putt.

Life does not provide such visible moments of high drama for most of us, but it does give many instances where we feel like we are in a vise. It is in these times that we find out a lot about our character. Our character is not what people see, but who we really are. Someone once said, "Character is not made in crisis—but only exhibited."

From the beginning, Moses expressed doubts regarding leading the people of God. He complained of his inabilities and frequently shared his concerns, from the time he received his

Day 12 | Is It in You?

commission. I am sure that the murmuring and complaints of the people only further served to reinforce Moses' desire to abandon his newly appointed leadership position.

The pericope above is one of the most well known in the entire Bible. Moses has led the Israelites out of bondage and on the road to freedom. However, he has run into a small obstacle, the Red Sea is in front of him. A further complication is that Pharaoh's army is behind him, ready to beat, maim, kill and drag God's people back into slavery.

Moses boldly addresses the people in faith. He tells them three things. First, don't be afraid. Fear traps us into believing that our demise is inevitable. Second, he tells them that God is going to work it out. Third, he tells them their enemies will be defeated and never seen again. These are bold statements of faith that are built on believing that God can do all things.

Faith believes, in spite of outward circumstances. This comes from allowing God to make a deposit of himself in us through study, prayer, fasting and meditation. When we are placed in life's vise and squeezed, either faith or fear will come out. Moses moved in faith. "Is It in You?"

Day 13

A Seat At the King's Table

The king asked, "Is there no one still left of the house of Saul to whom I can show God's kindness?" Ziba answered the king, "There is still a son of Jonathan; he is crippled in both feet."
Then Ziba said to the king, "Your servant will do whatever my lord the king commands his servant to do." So Mephibosheth ate at David's table like one of the king's sons.
II Samuel 9:3, 11

This morning while preparing for my day, I listened to the various news reports commemorating the 9/11 attacks. In watching, I was reminded of the many persons around the country who have clear wounds from 9/11, one of the most awful days in American History. I thought it appropriate to reflect today on a person from scripture who also carried clear wounds and might assist us as we begin this journey to wholeness.

I would like to take a look at a little known person in scripture named Mephibosheth. We know little about him except that he was one of Saul's sons. Saul, of course, was the first king of Israel who employed a young shepherd boy by the name of David to play on his harp to soothe the king's anger. Despite a very positive beginning, Saul eventually became jealous of the blessings bestowed upon David and attempted to kill him on several occasions. In spite of Saul's anger against David, he refused to kill the King on two occasions because he did not want to touch

Day 13 | A Seat At the King's Table

"God's anointed." Eventually Saul was killed in battle along with his son Jonathon, a beloved friend and brother to David.

In the text today, David has become king of Israel and wants to bless anyone from the house of Saul because of the kindness of his friend Jonathan. There remains only one relative, a son named Mephibosheth, who was crippled in both feet. I am wondering if you can imagine what it would be like to be crippled in both feet. I am sure that walking would be difficult. I am sure that he was shunned by other children because of his disability. I doubt that anyone picked him to play on their team on the playground. Even his very name, Mephibosheth, has a harsh sound to it.

What or who has wounded or crippled you in life? Your wounds may not be physical like Mephibosheth, but they are real. I recently read a quote by John Eldredge, who states, "Every person carries a wound. No matter how good your life may have seemed to you, you live in a broken world full of broken people." Eldredge is correct, everyone has wounds; but our wounds don't have to define us.

God moved on David's heart to remember his friend's son. David restored all of Saul's land to Mephibosheth. He assigned servants to work the land and bring the profits to Mephibosheth. Beyond that, David gave the prestigious honor of sitting at the king's table to an outcast.

I would have you to remember that Jesus was criticized for associating with the marginalized in society. He responded to such criticism by saying: "It is not the healthy who need a doctor, but the sick. I have not come to call the righteous, but sinners. " (Mark 2:17)

    Jesus came so that you and I could be healed from those things that cripple us. Like Mephibosheth, we are not deserving of such great honor, but we have been chosen. I pray that during this year you will hear God's call to you, to sit at the banquet table with Him.

DAY 14

KNOWING HIM

I want to know Christ and the power of his resurrection and the fellowship of sharing in his sufferings, becoming like him in his death.
Philippians 3:10

I have been blessed to know a lot of people in my life. There are some who I have been fortunate to develop lifelong friendships. I believe that I have the best friends that anyone could imagine. My friends insist on helping me when I fall and not allowing me to fail. True friendships are borne out through time and shared experiences. My best friend and I share similar backgrounds: we are the youngest in our families, our parents are from the South and married for over fifty years, we are graduates of the same high school and we have laughed, cried, hoped and dreamed together.

Friends are those persons that journey through life's ups and downs with us. I am sure many persons claim Jesus as their friend. This is a bold statement to be certain. I would like to take a moment to examine our claim. I would also have you to consider that pursuing excellence is impossible without knowing Him.

To know Christ means we have the humility to realize we are only in the relationship because he initiated it. That is because we are not worthy to have a friend who walks in integrity and honesty at all times. The gospel writer states, "You did not choose me, but I chose you and appointed you to go and bear fruit—fruit that will

Day 14 | Knowing Him

last." (John 15:16)

The growth of our relationship with Christ requires that we get to know him in an ever deepening and intimate manner. I once had a church member tell me, "I am still getting by on my momma's prayers." Intimacy requires a devotional and prayer life that is modeled after the one Jesus had with his Father. (Mark 1:35) It also requires that we stand for Christ even if we are persecuted. This is what Paul meant when he wrote about sharing in the fellowship of his suffering. Whenever we go through hardships with someone, there is the potential to strengthen the relationship.

Knowing Christ gives us the benefit of sharing in his inheritance. We share not only in Christ suffering, but also in the power of his resurrection. I believe it is important to note that this is not an either/or proposition. It is both. It is an inclusive statement. We can't have the blessing without the burden of standing as one of his disciples. When we share in his inheritance, "God will do exceedingly and abundantly beyond all that we ask or think according to his might power that is at work in us." (Ephesians 3:20)

In closing, I would have you consider my friends from the Peanuts gang. On one occasion, Peppermint Patty said to Marcie: "I'd like to read this book, Marcie, but I'm kind of afraid. I had a grandfather who didn't think much of reading." She continued by saying, "He always said that if you read too many books, your head would fall off." Marcie responds, "You start the first chapter, and I'll hold onto your head!" You may feel like everything is coming apart by the seams, but what a joy to know Christ. He won't let your head fall off.

DAY 15

Letting Go and Moving Forward

I want to know Christ and the power of his resurrection and the fellowship of sharing in his sufferings, becoming like him in his death.
Philippians 3:10

When we last left Jonah, he was in a holding pattern. This is like being on an airplane and the pilot announces over the speaker that "we are ready to touch down in Detroit." However, a few minutes later he comes back to tell you that due to some airport or runway condition, you will be circling the airport until this situation changes. I don't know about you, but I don't care for circling around the airport at twenty thousand feet.

The longer the holding pattern; the more we call on the name of the Lord. It is at times like this that we have the opportunity to reflect and think about what is important in life. So, we pray: God if you allow me to set foot on the earth again I am going to call someone I have been angry with and let them know I really love them. Dear God when this plane lands I am going to stop................

When we examine the summation of our lives, we realize that some of the things we hold so dear and special really are not that important, at all. Jonah had gotten into this situation because he had an attitude with God and was reluctant to share God's message of mercy with Jonah's hated enemies. Jonah determined

Day 15 | Letting Go and Moving Forward

that some persons were not worthy of God's love. He thereby made his way of thinking an idol, if you will.

An idol ultimately is anything that we put in the place of God. Sometimes they are referred to as sacred cows. We can make our morning routine into a sacred cow or an idol. I have to have the Today Show, my morning newspaper, Starbucks, Pepsi or Coke or a conversation with a friend. If anyone interrupts our routine we feel somewhat angry, moody and somewhat ineffective.

Any object of our devotion that replaces God is a lying vanity. It will fade away. It will not sustain us. It could be our ideologies or our denomination or what we have determined the church should or should not do. However, ultimately, the things that we hold so sacred outside of our love and obedience to God will ultimately fail us.

The sad thing here is the longer we hold on to these things the further we drift from God. There is someone today who is clinging, grasping, refusing to let go of a relationship that really ended a long time ago. It is our idealized understanding of life, whose fruit withered years ago, yet we cling to it. It has become worthless. It no longer provides joy, happiness or vitally. Then there are those occasions or things that attempt to cling to us. I pray that in either instance you would call out, "Lead me to the Rock that is higher than I." (Psalm 61:2)

The difficulties of life should ultimately cause us to cling and hold onto God. Let go of the past and seek what God wants for you. Shout and sing and make melody in your heart to the God of your salvation. If you look at your life, you will find that every time you needed help, God has stepped into the midst of your situation.

Letting go of "our way" prepares us for the perfection that God has in store for our lives. Perhaps I can help you to understand it in the following manner. The card game Bid Whist occasionally will deal one team with a perfect hand of cards. The excitement mounts for this team as they play each round of cards as they move towards running a Boston (i.e. as in Massacre). This means that they will win every book, much to the dismay of their opponents. However, as they approach the last cards, an opponent claims that they have reneged on a previous round. Why? They did not play the appropriate card at the right moment.

I don't know about you, but I don't want to forfeit the blessings that God has for me. French priest Jean-Pierre Caussade wrote in *The Joy of the Saints* "To escape the distress caused by regret for the past or fear about the future, this is the rule to follow: leave the past to the infinite mercy of God, the future to his good providence; and give the present wholly to his love by being faithful to his grace."

DAY 16

LISTENING IS AN ACT OF LOVE

Understand [this], my beloved brethren. Let every man be quick to hear [a ready listener], slow to speak, slow to take offense and to get angry.
James 1:19 Amplified Bible

I like to listen. I have learned a great deal from listening carefully. Most people never listen.
Ernest Hemingway

If the person you are talking to doesn't appear to be listening, be patient. It may simply be that he has a small piece of fluff in his ear.
Winnie the Pooh (by A.A. Milne)

Last week, I mentioned that we sometimes hear but don't always listen. This is equivalent to the saying "In one ear and out the other." Hearing, along with taste, touch, sight and smell make up our five senses. The word "listen" is actually defined as, "To make an effort to hear something." Therefore, listening involves the engagement of the person being spoken to.

This thought seemed to follow me around this past week and is highlighted in the book titled "Listening is An Act of Love." The authors are the architects of a project called StoryCorps. Story-Corps begin with a booth in New York City where everyday Americans could stop in with a loved one and receive a set of scripted questions. They in turn chose several questions and simply pre-

Day 16 | Listening is An Act of Love

sented them to an aunt, cousin, father or sibling. The responses provided rich depth and understanding of the human spirit.

I would suggest that modern technology moves us further apart instead of bringing us together. We are isolated in front of our computers and big screen televisions. We spend time with our IPods and MP3 players, but rarely with each other. This causes us to miss out on the rich vibrancy of listening to one another's story.

We are often in conflict with others because we fail to listen. These misunderstandings lead to blow-ups, becoming angry and "giving someone a piece of our mind" (as an aside, I am trying to hold on to my entire mind; giving some away is not an option). Deep chasms form and friendships, marriages and community are sometimes irreparably damaged.

Instead, I would suggest that we take Winnie the Pooh's advice and remove the fluff from our ears. We would find love and peace, if we did.

DAY 17

MORE THAN YOU EXPECTED

13But the angel said to him: "Do not be afraid, Zechariah; your prayer has been heard. Your wife Elizabeth will bear you a son, and you are to give him the name John. 14He will be a joy and delight to you, and many will rejoice because of his birth, 15for he will be great in the sight of the Lord. He is never to take wine or other fermented drink, and he will be filled with the Holy Spirit even from birth. 16Many of the people of Israel will he bring back to the Lord their God. 17And he will go on before the Lord, in the spirit and power of Elijah, to turn the hearts of the fathers to their children and the disobedient to the wisdom of the righteous—to make ready a people prepared for the Lord."
Luke 1:13-17

I am fond of the Lexus car commercial for Christmas. You know; the one where someone opens their eyes and their spouse dangles the key to the new car in front of them. The car is sitting in the driveway with a big bow on it. I think most of us would be happy with a present like that.

This caused me to wonder what if God interrupted your daily routine with an earth shattering announcement. Luke's account of the coming of our Lord offers two such accounts. Today, we will look at the story of Zechariah.

Zechariah was a faithful priest in the temple of the Lord. He

Day 17 | More Than You Expected

and his wife Elizabeth had no children and were well along in years. We find him simply going about his nine to five when he is confronted by the angel Gabriel, with news that is too amazing to comprehend.

The announcement is that Zechariah and Elizabeth will bring forth a child. That news alone was enough to leave Zechariah on the floor in disbelief. The angel goes on to tell him that the child his wife will bring forth will be a prophet to Israel. In disbelief, Zechariah laughed.

I believe that there are times when we, as readers of Scripture, are unfair to the persons that we are reading about. How could Jacob be so deceitful? Why did the Israelites disobey God again and again? How could David be the "apple of God's eye" yet falls into adultery? I believe as we focus through the lens of our own experiences, we can certainly relate and understand why Zechariah did not believe Gabriel's announcement.

However, we must always consider that there are consequences to our actions. Gabriel was very clear and not amused by Zechariah's response. "I stand in the presence of God." "You will be silent and not able to speak until the day this happens, because you did not believe my words, which will come true at their proper time."

God speaks to us in many different ways. Perhaps you have not experienced an angel speaking directly to you, but there are moments that God speaks to us directly or through others as his chosen vessels and the message is very clear. In those instances, we often wonder was that God, me, or did someone add some Christmas cheer to the office punch? And God, if it was you, what on earth did you mean? What am I to do?

We can understand Big Z's confusion and doubt. However, we must not allow doubt to move into fear. This can cause paralysis at just the moment that God is preparing to perform a miracle in our life. When we doubt the move of God, we could miss the blessings or peace he has for us.

I don't know that you will get the keys for a Lexus this year, but I pray that you will remember God is still able to perform miracles. I am praying that God will meet you at your point of need and provide you with what you are seeking. Move forward in faith knowing that he is "able to do exceedingly and abundantly more than we ask or imagine, according to his power that is at work within us." (Ephesians 3:20)

Day 18

On Peace

Let us therefore make every effort to do what leads to peace and to mutual edification.
Romans 14:19

Advent is the period of expectant waiting and preparation for the celebration of the Nativity of the Christ. It is a season of miracles and new beginnings. We reflect on the possibility for change and wonder if we have reached a moment in human history where man might choose to study war no more.

President William Jefferson Clinton said, "The real differences around the world today are not between Jews and Arabs; Protestants and Catholics; Muslims, Croats, and Serbs. The real differences are between those who embrace peace and those who would destroy it; between those who look to the future and those who cling to the past; between those who open their arms and those who are determined to clench their fists." The question must be asked, "What causes our fundamental differences anyway?"

I would suggest the differences are rooted in the individuals' desire to have his or her rights. Howard Thurman describes this in the seminal book "Disciplines of the Spirit." Thurman writes:
"When the baby comes, the entire household is reorganized and a new timetable of family activities created. For such a baby the time interval between wish and fulfillment is, in effect, zero.

Day 18 | On Peace

The baby expresses his wishes in a universal language—crying. As the baby grows older and is more and more an accepted part of the household, the sure signs of a counterrevolution begin to emerge. The time interval between the baby's cries and the adult response begins to widen. Now, quite properly, the duties of the household, the demands of other children and/or other members, all tend to introduce a kind of delayed action on the part of the mother. The immediate reaction of the child is clear and precise: varying forms of protest from the sustained whisper to the roaring scream."

The baby's desire is to have their right or wishes fulfilled at a time interval of zero. This same desire carries into adult life for many and when things don't go their way, the spiritually immature person reverts to a tantrum by "telling someone off," "blowing their top," or "giving them a piece of my mind." The individual uses all within their power to bend the will of others to their desires. Thurman suggests on a larger scale, this is what happens when one nation goes to war against another. The desire for national fulfillment must be met immediately or armed conflict is inevitable. National rights are more important than what is right.

Paul wrote to the Roman church about individual freedoms. There were some who argued over the right to eat certain foods. These foods may have been used in idol ceremonies and then resold on the market. Arguments broke out in the church. Some who were strong in the faith believed it was their right to eat or drink whatever they pleased. There were others who disagreed. These polar positions caused disagreements and sometimes tested the faith of those who were weak.

Paul admonished believers to do everything possible to encourage peace and to strengthen others. The institution of petty rules, personal dislikes, and cultural bias causes conflict and separation. We must be sensitive to others who will be harmed by our actions and sacrifice our freedom in Christ to encourage others.

Someone wrote, "We shall never have physical disarmament until we have succeeded in effecting moral disarmament." As we reflect on the possibility for peace, let's choose to lose our right to be right.

Day 19

Patience

But those who wait in the LORD will renew their strength. They will soar on wings like eagles; they will run and not grow weary, they will walk and not be faint.
Isaiah 40:31

In Letters to a Young Poet, nineteenth century German poet Rainer Maria Rilke advises to "be patient towards all that is unsolved in your heart and to try to love the questions themselves," for gradually, "you will live into the answers." These words are easy to hear but harder to live by, as patience is a virtue in modern society that is rarely taught and less frequently practiced.

We pray that we can move towards a place of authentic existence, yet we are frustrated over our present situation. We languish in holding patterns as our human inadequacies separate us from our divine destinies. The cry of humans' longing for completeness and affirmation is stomped in the face by deficiencies, transience and emptiness due to societies changing flux of values and standards.

I wish that for you and I, there was some easy answer to the myriad of situations that face our common dilemmas. I find myself in constant wonder over my existence and path in life. It would seem that as we watch wildfires destroy homes in California and reflect on the continuing deleterious effects of Hurricane Katrina,

Day 19 | Patience

this would cause thanksgiving to rise in our hearts.

However, the immediacy of our own existential situation defines our reality. Our moment in time seems to be the only one that matters in the universe. The timeless words of Isaiah can assist us with the multiplicity of questions that invade our lives. We must simply wait. It seems that minutes become hours, and days become weeks; but we must wait.

Our waiting should not be an idle matter. It involves seeking God with the little strength that we can muster. It means trusting God with all our heart, soul and mind. It means that today we will try to do better than yesterday. It means that we believe that God rewards those that seek after Him. Bills will mount, health will decline but we must wait on the Lord.

I urge you to embrace life today. Embrace it even with its twists, turns, trials and contradictions. Life's questions will be answered as we wait patiently on God. He will fulfill His promises and renew our strength.

Day 20

Staying on Track

Peter turned and saw that the disciple whom Jesus loved was following them. (This was the one, who had leaned back against Jesus at the supper and had said, "Lord, who is going to betray you?") When Peter saw him, he asked, "Lord what about him?" Jesus answered, "If I want him to remain alive until I return, what is that to you? You must follow me."
John 21:20-22

It is true that many times the words and actions of others cause us to delay or reconsider our actions; however, I have also found that often it is not the action of others but my own actions that cause me to become sidetracked.

I am wondering if it is just me or have you occasionally found yourself in the rat race? That means trying to keep up with the rest of the world and being influenced by its values and mores. The problem with looking at what others are doing is that it moves us away from reaching the goals and objectives that we have set for ourselves. Or more importantly, it is when we have heard directly from the Lord and we are sidetracked because of looking at someone else.

Of all the apostles, you just have to love Peter. He is up one moment and down the next. In Peter, we see courage and cowardice, strength and weakness, or as Jim McKay stated in the opening voice-over for ABC's Wide World of Sports, "The triumph of vic-

Day 20 | Staying on Track

tory and the agony of defeat." Peter has the faith to walk on water, but also to sink when he takes his eyes off of Jesus.

It is often where we look that causes us to get off track. In horse racing each horse has blinders, or winkers attached to a piece of horse tack on a horse's bridle that restricts the horse's vision to the rear and, in some cases, to the side. You see, horses have a 350 degree field of vision and are easily distracted.

Jesus has been addressing Peter about his calling and purpose. Peter looks around and sees the "Beloved Disciple" and wants to know "What about him?" Jesus speaks directly to him and states "You must follow me."

Have you lost focus on God? That is, have you looked over to the side? Hebrews 12:2 might help us; it reads, "Let us fix our eyes on Jesus, the author and perfecter of our faith, who for the joy set before him endured the cross, scorning its shame, and sat down at the right hand of the throne of God."

Today, this day, get back on the treadmill; say no to your good friends Ben and Jerry; stop right now and pray or read your Bible. Don't look to the right or to the left, stay on track.

Day 21

Singing Your Song

Let the word of Christ dwell in you richly as you teach and admonish one another with all wisdom, and as you sing psalms, hymns and spiritual songs with gratitude in your hearts to God.
Colossians 3:16

I have shared in several devotions of the rich legacy of my father, Pops. I have not written about my Mom. My family is blessed to have our mother with us. I have often said that if you were to look up the word "Christian" in a dictionary you would find my mother's picture next to it. The foundation of my faith has been taught to me in precept and example by my mother. One of the ways she has always done this is by singing.

My mother is always singing. She sings while she cooks. She sings while she washes and folds clothes. She sings while she reads the Bible. I always remember my mother singing. I can hear her now singing her favorite hymn, "I Come to the Garden Alone." She has a nice voice though she has never been in a choir. Unfortunately, my singing is a cross between Kermit the Frog and Bugs Bunny. She lovingly calls my best friend; her singing preacher.

I mention this because I am finding myself more often singing the hymns of the church when I'm awake, while driving or folding clothes. No one is there to hear how off key or flat my singing is except for the Lord. However, that is fine because God is not

Day 21 | Singing Your Song

concerned about our proficiency, but our profession of faith.

Paul encourages God's people to allow God's Word to dwell in them richly. This is like when a dish such as chili or spaghetti is allowed to sit for a day or so after preparation; on the next day, the seasoning that has been used blends together to create an even more appealing taste to the palate.

When we dwell on God's Word, it will remind us of principles to live by and strengthen our inner being. It will also bring to remembrance songs that have been meaningful to us on our journey. These songs will remind us of how good God has been and continues to be. So I suggest you meditate on God's Word, sing your song, be thankful to Him and watch your faith soar to new heights.

Day 22

Surrender

But whatever was to my profit I now consider loss for the sake of Christ.
Philippians 3:7

My sainted Sunday school teacher Ms. Zelpha Jones always made us sing what I thought was the saddest hymn in the church. At some point, each Sunday we would have to sing "I Surrender All." For those who are not familiar with the chorus, it is "All to Thee my blessed Savior, I surrender all." For most of us, this is more easily sung than lived. Our human nature desires to be in control. We seek to control our lives through the sum total of our finite experiences which are limited at best.

The Apostle Paul had every reason to believe that he should stay in control of his life. He chronicles in the third chapter of Philippians his pedigree, which would be equivalent to a Harvard Law Degree. He is clear that what he has attained is minimal to his faith in Christ. Too often, we only "trust in the Lord with all our heart" when we can handle life with the resources at hand. Trusting God means we will give our lives to Him, not just in moments of convenience and comfort, but also when obstacles and oppression confront us.

Frank Laubach, a missionary to the Philippines in the early 1900s, hit rock bottom one night. Looking at his life's work, it

Day 22 | SURRENDER

seemed as if it all amounted to nothing. He and his wife had lost three children to malaria. Now, in his mid-40s, he was sick and had to sequester himself from his wife and only remaining child. He was completely alone. That's when he met God.

Imagine how shocking this must have been. He had been a Christian most of his life. He had given his life to Christ and he had taken the gospel to foreign nations. But in his moment of deepest despair, he finally realized that he could live in intimate communion with God through the Holy Spirit. In quarantine, he found the union he longed for all of his life. He began to keep a journal and wrote the following words sitting alone on a mountain.

> "The most wonderful discovery that has ever come to me is that I do not have to wait until some future time for this glorious hour. I do not need to wait for any grace. This hour can be heaven. Any hour for anybody can be as rich as God. For do you not see that God is trying experiments with human lives......As for me, I asked God, "How wonderful do you wish this hour alone with me to be?" And God answered convincingly, "It can be as wonderful as any hour that any human being has ever lived. I have not become satisfied yet. I am not only willing to make this hour marvelous, I am in travail to set you aflame with the Christ. How fully can you surrender and not be afraid?" And I answered, "Fill my mind with your mind to the last crevice. Catch me up in your arms, God, and make this hour as terribly glorious as any human being ever lived, if you will. I don't know how one could live if his heart held more than mine has held from Thee these past few hours."

Surrender | **Day 22**

He went on by saying,

"Clearly my job here is not to go to the town plaza and convince people to change their religious beliefs or to win a theological debate. My job is to live wrapped in God, trembling with His thoughts, burning with His passion. And my loved ones, that is the best gift you can give to the place where you live. You and I shall soon blow away from our bodies. Money, praise, poverty, opposition, these make no difference, for they will all alike be forgotten in a thousand years. But this Spirit, which comes to a mind set upon continuous surrender – this Spirit is timeless life."

To release ourselves to the Spirit of God moves us to a place where we will not concentrate on the temporal issues of life. There is richness in dwelling on the Christ that cannot be found in any material packing at Nordstrom's or Neiman Marcus. Surrender will lead to a newfound joy and strength as we transverse life's most difficult moments.

Day 23

Taking a Nap

In Joppa there was a disciple named Tabitha (which, when translated, is Dorcas), who was always doing good and helping the poor. About that time she became sick and died, and her body was washed and placed in an upstairs room....Peter went with them, and when he arrived he was taken upstairs to the room. All the widows stood around him, crying and showing him and the others clothing that Dorcas had made while she was still with them.
Acts 9:36, 37, 39

It just overcomes you. You are at your computer typing or sitting in front of the television when all of a sudden you find yourself looking at your eyelids. My father had a friend who often said, "That food goes straight to my eyes." A quick power nap, while frustrating for some, helps to provide energy and focus for others. There are some cultures where taking a midday siesta is an acknowledged part of the workday.

On the other hand, there is the nap that causes you to fall into a very deep sleep. You did not realize the amount of hours that you have put in at work. You find everything in life is running together as you attempt to balance spouse, children, exercise, work, spiritual discipline and an occasional moment of joy. Though needed, when awakening from this type of nap, it can cause a violent upheaval in one's spirit because you realize that you have missed

Day 23 | Taking a Nap

taking care of important business and the day is half spent.

A cursory glance of life shows that we have all taken one of these unplanned naps. I spoke with my best friend earlier today to wish him Happy Birthday. We reflected on our age and wondered how we got here so quickly. I said to him that if we reach the average age expectancy for black men that we are already in the late summer of our lives. This nap I speak of is unplanned. This nap can see hopes, dreams and aspirations vanish. This leaves us feeling that a part of us has died.

Tabitha was a woman who was always doing good things for others. She helped the poor and made clothing for those that were in need. The writer of Acts does not describe her illness but we are told that she became sick. She was a member of the early church and clearly used her gifts to take care of others. This sickness led to death and it grieved those who loved her.

The disappointments of life can leave us distraught and emotionally distressed. There is never an appropriate time to grieve. This time is unique to the individual. Grief that is left to fester leads to depression and despair. This can cause periods of time to move in fleeting fashion. We are left wondering where all the time went.

Peter hears of Tabitha's condition and comes to visit with the grieving friends. He puts them all out of the room and prays for her. The Psalmist writes that "deep calls unto deep." The Spirit of God speaks gently to Tabitha and she sits up. She is a miracle for her friends to behold.

Taking a Nap | Day 23

God is speaking to you as you read this devotional. Healing and resurrection are taking place in your spirit. I believe that you are feeling peace and tranquility. That is because the Good Shepherd has awakened you from your nap. He is leading you to quiet pools and lush meadows. It may have been meant for evil but God meant it for good. You didn't plan to fall asleep as long as you did. You may be in late summer, fall or even the winter of your life. There is no need for anxiety; God has abundance for you today.

Day 24

Test Time

Examine yourselves to see whether you are in the faith; test yourselves. Do you not realize that Christ Jesus is in you—unless, of course, you fail the test? And I trust that you will discover that we have not failed the test.
2 Corinthians 13:5, 6

The thought of taking tests still terrifies the minds of many of us who have been out of the classroom for some time. The proper or best way to prepare for a test is to develop a regular discipline of study leading up to the test. This will take away some of the stress and anxiety of the big day. For too many of us, taking a test or exam involved staying up into the wee hours of the morning and cramming for the next day's event. If you are like me, you would probably rather forget the test result or certainly the agony of long nights of study.

Life is actually one big test, after another. There are times when we are able to prepare for the test i.e., a work deadline; and others, such as sudden illness or the loss of a loved one, that come without advanced notice. The ability to succeed in taking tests in a school setting is intricately tied to one advancing to the next grade.

However, the Apostle Paul speaks not of someone else administering the test, but us giving the test ourselves. He suggests that

Day 24 | Test Time

this test will prove whether or not we are Christians. Jesus said that "He (God) causes his sun to rise on the evil and the good, and sends rain on the righteous and the unrighteous." (Matthew 5:45) This tells us that we will have our good and great days, but also some days that test our faith.

Perhaps, as you face a test of faith, you might consider the following story. In 1924, two climbers were part of an expedition that set out to conquer Mount Everest. As far as it is known, they never reached the summit; and they never returned. Somewhere on that gigantic mountain they were overpowered by the elements and died. After the failure of the expedition, the rest of the party returned home. Addressing a meeting in London, one of those who returned described the ill-fated adventure. He then turned to a huge photograph of Mount Everest, mounted on the wall behind him.

"Everest," he cried, "We tried to conquer you once, but you overpowered us. We tried to conquer you a second time, but again you were too much for us. But, Everest, I want you to know that we are going to conquer you, for you can't grow any bigger, and we can!" It is not known if this climber ever made it, but years later Sir Edmund Hillary and his Sherpa guide Tenzig Norgay did.

Here is the good news for the day. You may have failed to reach the top before, but God is allowing you to take the test again. I pray that as you face your test of faith that God provides you with the endurance to reach the summit.

DAY 25

THE FAITH FACTOR

Jesus said to them, "Only in his hometown, among his relatives and in his own house is a prophet without honor." He could not do any miracles there, except lay his hands on a few sick people and heal them. And he was amazed at their lack of faith.
Mark 6:4-6

There is much discussion and debate surrounding the release of the movie, "The DaVinci Code." One of the early clues to the Code is called "The Fibonacci Sequence." This famous mathematical equation states that there is a progression in which each term is equal to the sum of the two preceding terms.

This caused me to think and question; can we describe faith in terms of an equation? The initial answer is no. Faith cannot be reduced to one plus one equals two. However, I do think we can examine looking at some building blocks that factor into our faith.

I believe that the first thing for us that we have to consider is; who is Jesus to you? Those in his hometown simply considered him to be a carpenter. Others looked at his family lineage and declared that he was nobody special. However, the Roman centurion who was not of the Jewish faith declared at his death, "Surely this man was the Son of God!"

Then there is the issue of pride. We are adults and we know

Day 25 | The Faith Factor

how to handle life or, so we think. The first sport I grew to love was baseball because of my grandparents. On a hot summer day, we sat on their enclosed back porch and listened to the game on the radio. A skilled pitcher understands that it is not how hard you throw the ball, but adjusting the speed on the pitch that causes the batter to strike out.

You see life changes speeds on us. There are times when we swing early, and times when we swing too late. We keep swinging and we miss hitting the ball time and time again. Our pride does not allow us to ask for assistance from the One who can help us hit the ball.

Ultimately, there is the issue of trust. I would have you consider the African impala. It can jump to a height of over 10 feet and cover a distance of greater than 30 feet. Yet, they can be kept in an enclosure in any zoo with a three foot wall. The animals will not jump if they cannot see where their feet will fall.

The philosopher Kierkgaard described it as the "leap of faith." Jesus was only able to touch and heal minor illness. Miracles can only happen when we honor Jesus as the Christ, the Son of the Living God. We must come to realize that we don't have the resources in our finitude to live life victoriously.

If there are any factors that I could add up for you, I would suggest the releasing of pride plus trust plus faith equals a miracle. It has been said, "Faith is a journey not a destination." I can hear strains of the saints of old singing, "Only believe, only believe all things are possible if you only believe."

DAY 26

THE MOUNT CARMEL BLUES

Elijah was afraid and ran for his life. When he came to Beersheba in Judah, he left his servant there, while he himself went a day's journey into the desert. He came to a day's journey into the desert. He came to a broom tree, sat down under it and prayed that he might die. "I have had enough, LORD," he said. Take my life; I am no better than my ancestors."
I Kings 19:3-4

I am not sure what triggers the feeling, but it always seems to happen when I have preached the gospel of Jesus Christ with all my God given strength. It happens when I have given the best that I have and I am drained. For some reason, it is then when I slowly begin to experience a kind of sinking feeling. I can't describe how and when it grabs me. I simply know there is a sadness that is sometimes very heavy.

    I thought about this on Monday morning after preaching for a friend's Pastoral anniversary. I have raised this issue with several friends in ministry and they have experienced it as well. It occurs after Sundays and preaching revivals. I call it "The Mount Carmel Blues." As I further considered my feelings, I found that Martin Luther battled constantly against doubt and depression. He once wrote, "For more than a week Christ was wholly lost to me. I was shaken by desperation and blasphemy towards God."

    Elijah was one of the greatest prophets in the Bible. He was

Day 26 | The Mount Carmel Blues

a dedicated and devoted servant of the LORD during a difficult period of Israel's history. King Ahab was easily influenced by his wife Jezebel, and the worship of false gods (Baal) was allowed and acceptable. Elijah challenged Ahab's leadership and demanded a showdown on Mount Carmel with 450 prophets of Baal. (I Kings 19)

Elijah called on the name of the Lord in the midst of overwhelming odds (450-1) and God did what he always does. He showed up and he showed out. You would think this would have left Elijah confident and glowing. However, Jezebel threatens Elijah's life and he sulks into fear and depression.

I believe the "Mount Carmel Blues" comes by to visit us in the midst of what should be our greatest moments of joy with the LORD. They don't just come by to visit preachers, but all those who love God and have done the best that they can. They come by to visit single mothers raising their children alone, children caring for an elderly parent, and students trying to do their best in school. They visit the faithful spouse, dedicated employees and the marginalized in society who watch the rich get richer.

The Mount Carmel Blues causes us to join in with Muddy Waters and B.B. King to write our own verses as painful details and brutal experiences ache within our consciousness of real or imagined pain. Elijah screamed at the threat of Jezebel that, "I have done my best and clearly my best is not good enough." His existential dilemma caused him to contemplate the end of life, itself.

The occasional visitation of these moments of despair must not remain unchecked. Elijah, despite God's care and devotion, continued to complain. God spoke to Elijah, not in the spectacular, but in silence.

    I pray for you that if the Mount Carmel Blues are attempting to visit you, that you will listen for God's voice. Remember, when fear is left unattended, it can grip us and carry us into a state of depression. Someone once stated, "Fear is conquered by action. When we challenge our fears, we defeat them. When we grapple with our difficulties, they lose their hold upon us. When we dare to face the things which scare us, we open the door to freedom."

Day 27

The Power of One

As he looked up, Jesus saw the rich putting their gifts into the temple treasury. He also saw a poor widow put in two very small copper coins. "I tell you the truth," he said, "this poor widow has put in more than all the others. All these people gave their gifts out of their wealth; but she out of her poverty put in all she had to live on."
Luke 21:1-4

Her name is Granny D. From January 1, 1999 to February 29, 2000, Granny D famously walked across the continental United States starting in southern California and eventually making her way across the country in support of campaign finance reform. She sometimes walked as far as eleven miles a day. When she arrived in West Virginia to unseasonable snow fall, she sent for her cross country skis. (If nothing else, I pray that you are inspired to exercise for thirty minutes today as recommended by most physicians).

Upon arriving in Washington, D.C. while lawmakers deliberated, she sometimes walked around the Capitol building for entire twenty-four periods only taking a bathroom or snack break. She tirelessly visited with Congressmen and Senators to regulate campaign finance reform. Ethel Doris Haddock, Granny D, began this journey when she was eighty-nine years old.

Day 27 | The Power of One

Our country seems to be filled with numerous vices and unaddressed societal issues that often leave us frustrated. We see corporate scandals everywhere and the rich get richer while the poor get poorer. Marvin Gaye described it by singing "Make me wanna holler, throw up both my hands." A good shout or holler is medicinal in the midst of that moment, but it does not eradicate the situation at hand. I would suggest that we should seek God's guidance to see how we can address the issue.

The woman in the text is often used as an example of good Christian stewardship. Her trust in God is unquestioned. To be a widow in antiquity with no husband or family placed you at the lowest rung of socio-economic existence. This reality did not deter the direction of this woman's decision. She was one woman, but I'm sure she believed that her giving would make a difference.

Jesus noted that all the others gave out of their wealth. What did he mean by that? Perhaps you remember the old hymn "Count Your Blessings"? Have you counted yours today? The songwriter wrote, "Count your blessings, name them one by one, count your many blessings, and see what God has done."

If you started counting, you probably would be unable to finish reading this short devotional. We may not be rich but we live in abundance. My point is simply that the average American has more than enough. I am sure it might not seem that way to you, but talk to refugees in Darfur, Sudan or residents of Bagdhad.

You and I have the power to make a difference. The key is that we must be passionate about affecting change in our families, community and our world. The Word of God is filled with the stories of Moses, Gideon, Esther and Amos, all of whom had their personal reasons to shirk into the background and fade to black. In fact, Scripture teaches, "Brothers and Sisters, think of what you were when you were called. Not many of you were wise by human standards; not many were influential; not many were of noble birth. But God chose the foolish things of the world to shame the wise; God chose the weak things of the world to shame the strong." (I Corinthians 1:26-27)

    I don't believe that one person can do it alone, but I do believe we can all make a difference. Edward Everett Hale, the distinguished poet and former Chaplain of the U.S. Senate, eloquently captured the essence of every American's duty: "I am only one, but I am one. I cannot do everything, but I can do something. What I can do, that I ought to do. And what I ought to do, by the grace of God, I shall do."

Day 28

The Roundabout Way

When Pharaoh let the people go, God did not lead them on the road through the Philistine country, though that was shorter. For God said, "If they face war, they might change their minds and return to Egypt." So God led the people around by the desert road toward the Red Sea. The Israelites went up out of Egypt armed for battle.
Exodus 13:17, 18

Life is an amazing journey. Each of us has experienced up and downs; days of sunshine and rain. Occasionally as we move along, we feel as though we are on a trip where we are following the directions we were given; yet there are detour signs that have added several extra hours to our trip. If we are honest, there are even moments where we feel lost. The detours of life cause us to take notice and have experiences that we would not have had if we had taken the direct route to our destination. Of course you remember from your Geometry class that the shortest distance between two points is a straight line.

I have a question for you, "Are you at the place in life that you said you would be five, ten or twenty years ago?" When I completed an undergraduate degree in Economics, my dream was to have a major six figure salary, a condo overlooking Central Park in New York and travel the world. Then, my life's trajectory was altered, due to a yearning inside of me to help others better themselves.

Day 28 | The Roundabout Way

I have of course wondered what would have happened in my life if I had made some different choices. This is something we have all contemplated at different times. I am sure that you have an occasional musing of the other job you could have taken, the engagement proposal you turned down, the business you could have started or the degree program you delayed. We often feel frustrated that we have not been able to take a more direct path to success as defined by the world.

Well, here is the good news for today. I believe that whatever path you have taken, if we follow the admonition of Isaiah "to seek the LORD while he may be found and call upon Him while he is near," that God is able to cause all grace and favor to abound to you.

The story of the Israelites' exodus from Pharaoh is known even to the most casual Bible student. If not, you may know it from the Hollywood production of the Ten Commandments. God's people are freed from slavery and oppression, only to have Pharaoh's army at their back and the Rea Sea in front of them. It is seemingly an impossible situation.

The scripture reading tells us that this was God's plan. If they had taken a more direct route the Israelites would have faced the Philistine army; hardened warriors that would have inflicted pain, hardship, and suffering that could have broken their spirits. So God actually led them towards the Red Sea.

I am not suggesting that God forced us to make the choices and decisions in our past; however, I believe that as we face our

The Roundabout Way | **Day 28**

Red Sea situations of today, that God can perform a miracle in our midst. We may have taken a circular path to our present position, but we don't know how life would have transpired with another choice. We may have fainted or lost heart with the added pressures of what would be seen as success in other people's eyes.

Today provides a wonderful chance for us to draw close to God. I believe in the days to come as you trust God, new opportunities will open up for you. I look forward to celebrating with you on the other side.

DAY 29

THE SECOND HALF

The Lord blessed the latter part of Job's life more than the first.
Job 41:12

It pains a Detroit Pistons fan to acknowledge that the Boston Celtics are the 2008 NBA Champions. I am happy for two of my favorite players, KG (Kevin Garnett) and Ray Allen, but otherwise I'm a bit disgusted. The Celtics largely owe their championship to an incredible comeback victory in the fourth game of the series.

I was at my barber the day after the game. He commented that he could not believe that Boston was losing by so much in the first half. In the first half of the game the Celtics trailed the Lakers by twenty four points. He then said, "Yeah, you know those NBA games; it's the second half that's really important."

I thought about the comment my barber made as an excellent reflection on life. Circumstances sometimes pile on top of us and leave us so deeply buried that it seems we will always be on the losing end. The urge in these moments is to quit. The game is over. There really does not seem to be a reason to continue to play.

Job gives us an example of why we should continue, despite the odds. Job is described as the greatest man among his people in the Bible. Yet, through a series of unfortunate events, his children die, he loses all of his earthly possessions and he is stricken with

Day 29 | The Second Half

shingles. His wife suggests he should "Curse God and die;" while his friends were accusatory instead of comforting.

I believe that we can find ourselves victorious in the second half if we adhere to a couple of basic principles. I would suggest that you celebrate today. You might feel there is little to celebrate, but I would say the fact that you are reading this devotion is a reason to celebrate. You are still alive. You are breathing. God can call those things in existence that are not.

I am sure this is not the first time you have been behind in life. The same God that did it before can do it again. His nature is unchanging. His specialty is saving us in difficult situations. If you don't believe me, ask Moses, Daniel, or the three Hebrew boys.

Finally, when the home team is introduced at NBA games the crowd has been whipped into frenzy by the announcer. The captain of the team is always introduced last. As Christians, we have a captain. "Ladies and Gentlemen, he came from heaven to earth, to show us the way. Lets give it up for our captain, Jesus Christ. The game is not over; the second half just started. Be encouraged.

Day 30

Like Home

The desert and the parched land will be glad; the wilderness will rejoice and blossom. Like the crocus, it will burst into bloom; it will rejoice greatly and shout for joy. The glory of Lebanon will be given to it, the splendor of Carmel and Sharon; they will see the glory of the LORD, the splendor of our God. The burning sand will become a pool, the thirsty ground bubbling springs. In the haunts where jackals once lay, grass and reeds and papyrus will grow.
Isaiah 35:1-2, 7

I am a lover of traditional jazz. For me there is nothing like listening to Sarah, Ella, Miles and Trane. That being said I enjoy all forms of music. One of my favorites is listening to Stephanie Mills' heart-stopping, hair-raising, goose-bump inducing "Home." I usually have to hit the seek button several times, and listen again and again.

If you don't know some of the lyrics, she sings; "When I think of Home, I think of a place, Where there's love overflowing. I wish I was home, I wish I was back there, with the things I been knowing." Home for me is sitting with my Mom and being her baby. Nia, my daughter, the youngest grandchild is proud to be "the baby's baby." Home for me is visiting the church that nurtured me in the Christian faith, St. Stephen African Methodist Episcopal in Detroit. Home for me is catching up with old friends and laughing about all the fun experiences we have shared.

Day 30 | Like Home

The theme of home is central for many religious, faith traditions. This involves taking a journey. The Buddhists do this at every shrine, every able-bodied Muslim is taught to attempt at least one pilgrimage to Mecca, and first century Jews were required to travel to Jerusalem at least three times a year for the Feast of Passover, the Feast of Weeks, and the Feast of Booths.

The first time the people of Israel journeyed, it was from Egyptian slavery to the Promised Land. They became disillusioned, distressed and often unappreciative of God's goodness. This brought unnecessary experiences of thirst and hunger. The present journey described by the prophet Isaiah from Babylon to Zion causes him to see flowers and parched earth. Isaiah also saw dry sand became pools of water and springs of life. The Israelites' journey had been consecrated and blessed.

Similarly, the journey during the Christmas season is a mix of emotions for some. Many travel by car, bus, train, and plane to see loved ones, celebrate traditions and rejoice because of God's blessings during this year. However, as some celebrate, others will have moments of depression, loneliness and sadness. This year has had many ups and downs for them. Some will mourn because they are without a beloved family member that has made their transition.

I pray that wherever the journey of life has taken you this year, that you might be at home. Home is not only a physical destination but home is to know Immanuel. That is, God is with you. You will experience being at home when you know that he will still walk with you and talk with you along life's narrow way. You will

Like Home | **Day 30**

experience home when as Stephanie Mills sings you know that you are in "A world full of love." Because no matter how rough the journey has been God has never left you, nor forsaken you.

Isaiah's words speak to us that in the midst of life, God's glory is being revealed in ways that we do not perceive. You don't have to wish. God wants to pour his overflowing love into your life. When you take a moment to reflect on God's presence, it will bring you peace. You then will be certain there is no place like home.

If you have comments or wish to contact the author for speaking engagements, Reverend Moore can be reached at **dsmmin@msn.com**